Beauty surrounds you
everywhere !

Charles Leahy

The Beautiful Way of Life

Charles Lelly

UNITY BOOKS
Unity Village, Missouri

Cover photograph by Keith McKinney. Black and white photographs by M. Jean Cox (pp. 12, 27, 46, 62, 65, 75, 78, 106, 123, 134, 141) and Keith McKinney (pp. 30, 41, 49, 81, 85, 150).

Table of Contents

Introduction

Words Are Only Guidelines

BEAUTY CAN be physical, spiritual, mental—and sometimes all three.

"The beautiful way of life" is a philosophy, a religion, a discipline, a harmony—all of which are directed to expansion of our individual awareness and finally to fulfillment of our divine potential.

Emphasis is placed upon the right use of our physical senses, with the expectation that this will lead us to experiences beyond the physical—into dimensions that may be mysterious and difficult to describe in words, but nevertheless deeply soul-satisfying and real.

Meditation and silence are always expected, because these are highways to soul experiences. Even though our starting point may be the consideration of ordinary things, our objective will be to go beyond the physical—to penetrate the object and find the source of its beauty, its form, its very existence!

I will write about experiences that transcend the

descriptive power of words. I will ask you to step beyond the symbolism of words into the source of words. Reading between the lines is essential. The words are only starting points for you, the reader, who can become the experiencer.

Always we will be pointing to something greater than the sum of its parts. The implication is that a mysterious wonder is embedded in every particle of the universe and that our purpose in living is constantly to increase our awareness of the Source of our being.

I will be writing about how to recognize this awe-inspiring experience, how to set the stage for its discovery, and how to keep on enlarging our view of it. Our search for the beautiful way of life will allow us literally to roam everywhere for methods or techniques. We will share experiences with the great mystics who found their way and have tried to convey its ineffability to us.

Our inquiry will lead us to questions about our state of being, our state of present living, and our state of becoming.

Another of our goals is freedom from bondage. Many of us are locked in by outworn traditions, erroneous educational conditioning, and even by our own fears of the unknown. Each of us needs to discover the wonder of being a unique entity in a universe of entities. Each of us is something special, and it is time we claim our birthright and be ourself—first, last, and always!

Only by first discovering the real worth of ourself can we begin to share anything worthwhile with others. We need to develop natural poise, self-confidence, and strength. Sharing is an integral part of life, and we need to know how to share. Otherwise we can never be fulfilled.

Balance is one word we will talk about frequently—a dynamic, not a static kind of balance. Balance plus awareness equal love, and this, too, will be an important aspect of our search.

Discriminating choice will be given a great deal of attention, because choosing the right incoming stimuli is of paramount importance. You should ask yourself many times: "What do I really want? Will it build me up or tear me down?" The art of discrimination makes the difference between grossness and fineness, vulgarity and elegance.

We'll travel together and discover the wonders that exist all around us. It will not be an easy trip, because I will expect you to be more than an armchair traveler. I will expect you to struggle for your own unfoldment . . . but I can truthfully say that if you sincerely want to enlarge your spiritual awareness and are willing to pay the price, the rewards of the beautiful way of life will be beyond your imagination.

—Charles Lelly

I.

Beauty
of
Being

Source, Alpha, Essence,

God, All Is Mind,

Beginning of Consciousness

Know Thyself

IN ORDER TO ACHIEVE the goal of dynamic balance in your life, you must know something about yourself. This knowledge must be distilled from your personal analysis, not the borrowed conceptual standards of some outside authority. You should be the authority for what you are at the moment. Who in the world can know as much as you do about you and your deepest feeling?

Most of our life we have been stuffed full of concepts, values, standards, approval and disapproval of others. This is normal and natural, and some of this input is desirable, helpful, and essential. By this method we save an enormous amount of time. In this way we learn quickly the concepts and skills that have been discovered and developed by humankind.

Unfortunately, we often fall into the trap of passivity. We assume that it all has been accomplished. We accept the past as right for us. Our values are usually generalizations distilled from the experience of time; they are often distorted, abused, sometimes no longer useful. We continue to accept conflicting views when we should be seeking our own specific guidelines.

At some time in our development pattern we need to call a momentary halt to the stuffing-in process and say, "I must now determine what is right and true for me as an individual!" In many cases we have had so little practice at being ourself that it becomes exceedingly painful to interiorize, to analyze our deeper self.

We have been led to believe that if we are not good children, we will be spanked. And spanked we are, over and over! Somehow we can never live up to the ideals set for us by others. We cannot accept any thought or action that does not conform to some artificial standard. We feel fear, guilt, inadequacy.

When we really begin to be completely honest with ourself, we see a scared individual lost on some unknown planet in a lesser known galaxy; we seem to be only a speck of dust on that planet. The vastness of the universe fills us with awe and fear. But we have been conditioned to accept the fear more readily than we do the awe and wonder of life.

When we begin to look for ourself, we must accept what we find, just as a scientist must accept what he sees under a microscope. What concerns us is not what we should be, but what we are at the moment. In most cases we have mistakenly accepted the fact that many of our basic feelings are evil, so we also accept the guilty feeling of not measuring up.

The more we discover about ourself, the more guilty we feel. We need to find ways of escaping this vicious trap. We need to be objective with ourself and look with the eyes of a nonjudgmental researcher. We need to know what we really are at the moment. If we do not like what we see, we should not collapse in fear and guilt, but earnestly resolve to begin choosing those actions that will make us conform to our own standards of behavior.

Is it insanity to allow people to be whatever they wish to be? As Shakespeare said, "To thine own self be true . . . Thou canst not then be false to any man."

I believe that when we accept ourself as we are and consciously choose what we wish to become, we will not only grow in strength and stature, but we will also become a light and an inspiration to others. When you catch a glimpse of the wonderful entity you are, you will be so full and overflowing that you will want the same for everyone else.

We need first to build an image of ourself that we can be proud of . . . an image that we strive ceaselessly to fulfill. At each step on the ladder of fulfillment we add a measure of substance that in turn radiates its purity and beauty to everything close to our magnetic force field. We literally radiate what we are at each moment in time to everything within range. If we are empty, mean, discouraged, greedy, these qualities are being sent out into the ethers. If we are full of love, aware of beauty, balanced in both body and soul, these qualities are transmitted.

What you are at this moment is radiating out from you to all 360 degrees of the spectrum. You may fool yourself, but you can't fool nature. Nature's laws operate whether you agree or disagree. Think about this for a moment: *I am radiating what I am at this moment.*

It can be a frightening thought; but if you resolve to look seriously, honestly, and objectively at what you are, you will realize that you differ only in minor degree from the world's greatest genius or most illustrious religious mystic. At this moment, resolve to begin to accept the full responsibility for your life. If you will begin to set your own standards for everything and allow me to set mine, we will never be too far apart in kind—only in degree. If you want more out of life than you have thus far achieved, you must declare your intentions and begin acting in accordance with your new insights.

You will struggle for accomplishment, but you will reach heights of joy you never thought possible.

The real struggle is not against an outside adversary, but against your passive acceptance of the notion that you are nothing. The struggle is basically aimed at breaking the hold that artificial standards have on you. Stop fighting outside forces and release yourself to a whole new way of life—a life that offers beauty, love, balance. Allow yourself to be, to become, and finally to surrender to a higher state of awareness wherein you see beauty that did not previously exist for you.

Ultimately you become the master of your own life and a co-creator of the ever-changing universe. You return consciously to your heritage—your infinite partnership with God.

The Great Mystery of Life

GOD REALLY is the great mystery of life! Our contact with the Infinite—God, Spirit, Source, or whatever else we may call it—is up to us as individuals.

The only thing that ministers, priests, writers, and/or counselors can do for us is to nudge us a little bit to stimulate our desire for growth.

Often we are given a quick affirmation by a well-meaning person, as though to suggest that saying it will immediately solve our current problem. I find that when I use an affirmation for myself it must somehow go so deep within me that it actually reaches every cell of my body. I must feel it; I have to know that I'm going to be a better person tomorrow, and the next day, and the next day. I think that when we imply that it is easy to obtain spiritual illumination, we are deceiving ourself and others.

There seems to be no such thing as discipline in today's society. It's a nasty word. You don't discipline your children anymore; you don't discipline yourself . . . you do anything you please!

Isn't it true that, in our self-growth, we have to say yes to this and no to that? Constantly, daily, every moment of our life we are making choices, and those choices add up to the kind of person we are right now. We can't take this away; we can't change it. I have to accept you just as you are; you have to accept me just as I am. I am a product of every choice I have ever made, whether conscious or unconscious, visible or invisible.

When we begin to ask ourself some really basic questions, we don't find easy answers. "Who am I?" There's a good question for you! You can work on that one for a thousand years. You can read a lot of books on theology, and still the answer eludes you. Or you might eventually come up with the answer, "I don't know." At least this is an honest approach. Historically, many mystics received illumination when they gave up in despair of trying to answer such questions.

We always have those around who can give an absolute statement about anything. Ask them, "What is God?" and they give you one, two, three, four, five, six, seven attributes—that's God! But if you look deeper than the words of these people, you will realize they are not what they say.

I had a conversation with a man recently, and if I had not been able to hear a thing he said, his message would have come to me clearly. His well-chosen words seemed to lack the ring of truth. With every body movement he made—his eyes, his gestures—he told me a very different story about the kind of person he was. If I had listened to what he said, without looking at the silent body language, I might have been led astray. What we say and what we are may be miles apart.

What are we really trying to do in life? We are trying to integrate what we are, what we say, and what we think. We are trying to put Humpty Dumpty back together again. We have fallen off the wall and been thrust out into this universe, and we don't know why.

We are trying to find our way home. We suspect that we already have what we are looking for. Nobody can give it to us!

All the books, all the discussions, everything else should finally result in our own private inquiry into what and who we are. That can be painful, because so often we don't know the answer, we don't have a solution now. But we slowly begin to build upon what we think, what we are, what we say to the world, and this finally reveals the infinite depth of our being.

As we grow in awareness and stature, surely each of us will finally arrive at the realization of Walt Whitman:

> *I know I am august;*
> *I know that I am deathless.*

Why the Search for Beauty?

RELIGION IS often treated as a much-too-serious part of our everyday life. Much of Christian theology has been concerned with sin, suffering, guilt, fear, and these attributes certainly do not appear to be beautiful. Somewhere the balancing qualities of awe, love, happiness, freedom, and confidence were de-emphasized.

Obviously negative qualities do exist in our nature, but so do positive qualities. We dare not choose one exclusive of the other. A dynamic balance between the constructive and destructive aspects of our nature should be maintained.

What is sadder than the person who is overwhelmed with a sense of sin or guilt? He brings only despair to himself and others. But almost as sad is the person who displays exaggerated enthusiasm, gaiety, effervescence. He bubbles his energies away uselessly.

Is not the mature person who balances the good and the not-so-good qualities of life to be admired and respected? He is aware of the rhythmic change of his dual nature. Usually he discovers that he can slip into the negative qualities of his nature almost effortlessly and that it takes considerable effort to accent the positive qualities. But this very effort produces strength and stamina for the enjoyment of the beautiful way of life.

When we say "the beautiful way of life" we include the totality of life experiences that we accept and mold to our own satisfaction. Beauty is really another term for the essence of God. This essence transcends the dualities, but is also immanent in every particle of our dual universe.

Beauty is the mysterious quality that shouts loudly, "Ah, this experience is right for me, now!" It is an abstract term that is difficult to define because it has a slightly different meaning for each of us. But I think we will agree that when we accept or experience beauty we intuitively know that life contains much more than we can comprehend. Beauty always suggests something beyond—something greater than ourself.

The search for beauty is a journey into the meaning of the universe. The experience of something beautiful is a reward for our perseverance. Beauty goes beyond the hardships of life and makes it all worthwhile. When beauty finally suffuses our soul, nothing else will take precedence, because we will have discovered the essence God.

The Hem of Reality

IT IS RARELY observed by those who are converted to a new form of religion that they have left their old set of words, concepts, ritual, and have accepted a new stage setting.

They often feel refreshed, renewed, and excited with the "new" ideas and terminology. In fact, they have exchanged the outer dress for new clothes. Sadly, this process is accepted as a great step forward with the feeling that "At last I have the perfect way of living."

It is so easy to delude oneself into believing that by changing the outer superficial self, the whole person can be permanently changed. If this were true we all would have found fulfillment long ago and mankind's ceaseless search would have ended.

The first symptom of the euphoria that follows the discovery of "the new way" is that the convert now wonders why he missed this simple process before, and also (which is more serious) why all his friends have not discovered such world-shaking truths! His next step may be to become a "one-man show" and try to change all sinners into saints overnight.

He has changed his outer garment and now wants everyone else to change clothes too! He is still trying to conform to a standard that he believes is the absolute truth. (This missionary zeal has been responsible for countless wars and strife since recorded history began, and continues to be responsible today.) He may think that since he has found "the way," his "new" ideal, any means of achieving this ideal is permissible.

This illusion ("my way is the only way") is seen in every sphere of life including philosophy, politics, economics, and sociology.

Many of us are so eager to find serenity or fulfillment that we fail to realize that we must go deeper. If we have merely changed clothes, we have only become fixated in a new mode. Growth and enlightenment never cease. We dare not allow ourself the luxury of contentment with another set of values. We must continue plumbing the depths of our being—questioning, observing, becoming aware of habitual patterns of thought that repeat the same errors over and over again.

"Know thyself" is easy to say, but hard to do. All such aphorisms are the same. If we become hypnotized by words and concepts and do not transcend these outer layers and find the reality hidden in the core of our being, we are only clanging cymbals and speaking inanities.

If we are quick to judge others because their outer garments are different from ours, we have not yet even touched the "hem of reality."

When we touch reality, even for a moment, we find that the ineffability of it defies description in words, concepts, ideas, values. It simply *is!* It cannot and will not be contained, bottled up, for easy distribution. It is available to everyone equally, but does not offer itself to egocentric individuals. It is universal.

The message here is simple: We can be aware of the Supreme Reality, but we cannot force awareness with outer disciplines. It is found only by inner attunement to the purity of being.

What's in a Thought?

IT IS STILL DARK when I arise. But the time before the sun arrives is so sweet, so friendly, so tranquil. Never does coffee smell so good, never is the mind so clear, never is God so near!

One morning recently it seemed to me that the thoughts we each have are our stock and trade in life. Most of us toss these assets to the winds. We rarely realize that our own thoughts are more precious, more useful, more authoritative for us personally than those of others. Somehow our culture conveys the idea to us that it is more blessed to study the thoughts of others than it is to study our own.

Creation is merely the freezing of our own thoughts.

Imitation is the acceptance of the crystallized thoughts of others.

This is not to say that the thoughts of others should not be sought. It is, however, a warning to balance the musings of others with our own.

It seemed to me on that particular morning that the essence of God centered every thought. We co-create with God. What a destiny!

Be it ever so humble, there's no thought like our own.

I asked myself, Who am I?

I am one of God's thinkers!

Where am I going?

Wherever my thinking takes me.

What am I?

I am the child of God's thinking. God thought me into existence, and I am thinking His grand-children into existence.

II.

Beauty
of
Awareness

Light, Form, Awakening,

Recognition, Awareness of Being

Moments of Reality

ONE OF THE miraculous things about the spring season is the ease with which we are able to focus our attention upon nature's never-ceasing movements. It is a time when the cyclical movement comes to the surface and we are almost forced into awareness of the renewal going on around us. It is a time when we can feel close to God more easily because His miracles are surfacing before our very eyes.

The first crocus that appears through the snow becomes a spiritual awakening, if only we realize it for what it is. We have been so conditioned that we believe spiritual experiences should be serious, churchy, abstract, or other-worldly. And yet, here is the face of God before us! Here is the wonder of life beckoning for our full attention. God is the crocus. God is the daffodil, the forsythia, the dogwood!

When we give our full attention to a single crocus, we have entered the holy ground of being.

God is manifested in every particle of the universe, but when we come upon the crocus we spontaneously become aware of our *own* holiness. There is communication between the ground of being in the crocus and the ground of being in us. It becomes a current that, if not resisted, produces a shower of light sparks that enfold us and radiate out from us. This may last only a second, but its impact is long-lasting.

This dynamic current of light is available to us all, but, unfortunately, we have resistors built in everywhere to prevent its free flow. Our past conditioning becomes a massive barrier to a living, moving, spiritual awakening.

We have been taught to rely so heavily upon our thinking mind that we literally are drowning in concepts, ideas, values, goals. We have been told that if we cannot put something into words, we don't understand it. How can words describe the ecstasy of the spontaneous happening when crocus and man become one?

We have around us a million opportunities each day to experience God directly, and yet we go looking for Him in the strangest places. We try to conceptualize Him. We try to enclose Him in structure. We try to imprison Him just as we have imprisoned ourself. What a pity!

We are locked up in a prison of our mind. We are walking through paths of wonder and awe, yet we are so busy trying to fit God into our own value systems (which have been mostly acquired from other imprisoned minds) that we see only dimly.

If we can take off the dark glasses and allow the natural light to pour through, we will not fret about our inability to express the miracle of life in words. We will accept reality naturally, without judgment. We will accept what is, not what should be! If we lower our defenses, eliminate our resistors, and begin to enjoy unencumbered, then God begins to shine through and we are lifted up to the high heaven of ecstasy. Even if this is only for one moment of our life, it makes life worthwhile. Why not allow this splendor to emerge and enjoy countless moments of reality?

Awake, O Sleeper

I REMEMBER that as a child I once looked through a knothole in a fence. As I peered through this opening into the unknown world on the other side, certain objects came into view quite distinctly; yet on the perimeter everything seemed out of focus.

When a friend and I were looking through separate knotholes, each of us would see something quite different. Each of us had a limited view of the other side; yet each would stoutly defend the fact that what he was seeing was true and declare that the other was in error and not seeing correctly. I might have said: "Can't you see that red wagon? I see it. I know it is there."

My friend might have said, "No, there is no wagon, only a horse."

If we children could have removed this visual barrier of the fence, we would both have recognized that each was correct in his description, but had described only part of the whole scene. Even at this point each would have seen slightly different things, since it is impossible for two persons simultaneously to have the same vantage point. But with a full view, at least the descriptions would be similar!

Looking through a knothole is such a simple, unsophisticated experience, but it has great depth of meaning for each of us. How often the simple things go unnoticed!

Each of us has an opening, or "knothole," through which he observes the cosmos. We each have been excited by what we see and we cry out to others: "Look, look, what I see! It is so beautiful, so colorful, so orderly—this is the truth. I see it! I can experience it! Why can't you see this? Can't you understand the truth? Are you so dull that you can't understand what is directly in front of you?"

This may be an oversimplification, but isn't it true that each of us is a solitary observer, distressed at the different descriptions coming from our fellows? How many times have you asked yourself: Am I sane? Am I stupid? Why don't I see what the others are seeing? Is there something wrong with me?

My mother says this thing is so. My teacher says this other thing is so. My minister says still another thing is so! I see this . . . and this . . . and this . . . but when I describe my observations to my associates, they rebel against them.

Am I so different from the rest?

If only we could strongly answer to the last question: *"Yes!* I am different from the rest and this is my greatest gift! I am unique. I am an individual. I must enlarge my vision to see more. Everything I see is so fascinating. Let me see more!"

The curious thing is, as we each widen the opening through which we are looking, we begin to have a greater range of vision. Then, and only then, we begin to recognize some of the objects described by other observers. We begin to have a kinship with many from whom we formerly were alienated because of their "narrow" views.

Isn't this analogy close to the situation in which every man and woman living in the world today finds him/herself? Aren't we constantly bombarded with laws, creeds, absolutes, formulated by others who say, "Believe as I do because *this is the truth"?*

Since birth we have been so persistently under attack to accept another's view that we have come to the point of being unable to look for ourself. We have relinquished our own cosmic view and timidly acquiesced to the "older, more experienced observer."

However, a few individuals out of the billions born on this planet refuse to do so—they refuse to accept any view without checking it out for themselves. They retain their cosmic right to their own views. They grow in awareness, and they regularly practice the art of viewing everything for themselves.

The world calls one of those select few a genius, a mystic, a Christ! He is sometimes misunderstood because he cannot accept the least-common-denominator view of the masses. And yet he stands out brightly above the rest as he gains added strength by removing any barrier to his widening vision. Soon he stands out like a star of the first magnitude. He is using his birthright and tirelessly enlarging his own knothole view of the cosmos. He becomes self-active and self-starting—a creator!

Another curious thing is that as his visual field enlarges, his capacity for understanding and love for other travelers along the way is also increased. He has lost nothing but his former limited or narrow visual range, and he has gained everything worth having. Isn't there a message here for each of us? How many of us persistently work to enlarge our knothole to the cosmos? How many of us long ago succumbed to the deadly persuasion of "one view of the universe"?

Have you ever looked at the Milky Way on a dark night and imagined yourself to be one of those stars? You are one, you know! Whether you will let your light shine brightly or hide it with artificial barriers is up to you. What a glorious awakening is in store for you when you realize that you are your own source of light, freely moving in the cosmos, subject only to the larger source out of which we all are made! What a stupendous opportunity!

"Awake, O sleeper." Claim your view of the cosmos—a view infinitely wider than your physical eyes reveal.

You are important to the cosmos. You belong. You have a source of help beyond your present awareness. The only permanent wealth is awareness of your source of Being. (All this is much more than a knothole view.) Everything that is needed for your continued development is already provided and awaiting your acceptance of your place in the cosmic scheme. As you become increasingly aware, your own light source becomes more and more visible to others—a star that lights the way!

How Are We Different?

IT SEEMS THAT WE are continually being deceived about the answer to the question, "What is the good life?" Those who have things to sell are vying for our attention with a staccato beat that is seemingly endless. Usually the message is, "If you accept my product, you will find the good life."

But most of us can remember how we dearly longed for a doll or a bicycle and earnestly believed that if we acquired that wonderful "thing," we would be content and eternally grateful. What a blow to our philosophy when the luster disappeared soon after the acquisition! Then we usually said, "If only I could have this new thing—then I would be happy."

After many such experiences we finally realize that fulfillment does not come by this method.

Obviously we need certain physical things to lift us beyond the survival level so that we can address ourself to such philosophical questions as, "What is the good life?'' Physical things are necessary to our well-being, but the fulfillment of our soul will not come through physical objects alone.

We must search deeper for the definition of the good life.

What really makes one person different from another? We all come out of the same Source; each of us has a physical body with built-in sense mechanisms; there are more similarities between us than differences. We human beings are strikingly alike. What then is the important difference between us?

It is the degree of awareness! One person sees with his soul; another sees only with his eyes and is relatively blind. One person drinks of the essence of spirit; the other gets the foam. The life of one person is a continuous experience of wonder and awe; the life of another is an experience of confusion and despair.

It would seem then that we should try to be more aware. This is not as easy as it sounds. Increased awareness is achieved more by relaxation than by action upon the objective world of things. Awareness is increased when we allow it to happen, more so than when we struggle to discover it.

Chronic ''busyness'' as we know it in our culture is not the seedbed of increased awareness. Perhaps we could start by practicing letting go and just being for a segment of time, allowing awareness to grow within us.

Why not tonight? Go outside, sit or lie on the ground, and quietly give yourself to the stars. Just observe. Do not judge, identify, or classify! Just be one entity in space looking at another entity in space. After a while you will realize that increased awareness silently slips into your consciousness when you least expect it.

It's so simple—but it works!

The Spiritual Dimension

THERE IS A spiritual dimension to each of us that is seldom reached even by so-called religious or pious people.

Religion today suffers as almost everything else does from "over-choice." Literally thousands of different sects vie for our attention by presenting cogent reasons for the supremacy of their particular ideology.

Such words as *reason* and *ideology* are in the realm of the intellect, of the reasoning mind. We see everywhere classes, discussion groups, encounter groups, all dealing with the *raison d'être* of their particular areas of interest.

We may also observe that our entire educational process, as it is conceived today, is primarily that of nurturing the intellectual aspect of our being. Many of us accept the concept that if we fill a young person's mind with all the "currently acceptable ideas," he will be educated, and that because he is educated in this manner, he will be a virtuous, kind person who will serve his fellow man. If this system really worked, the world today would not be an armed camp, as it certainly is.

Obviously we are not advocating the abolition of intellectual training. Everything begins as an idea of mind; this is universal law. The error lies in the belief that the development of the intellect is the goal. It is in reality only the tool that helps to pry open the vast inner universe of a person, wherein the spiritual dimension is made apparent.

The level of the intellect should be kept in perspective. It is an integral part of a larger ground of being.

The body, the mind, the soul—these are the aspects of our being. The body is cared for to provide the purest vehicle possible to enable the mind to be fully active and curious about our Source of being. When the physical body is brought into balance with a disciplined mind, one is ready to open the door of the soul that contains the spiritual dimension of man. Herein lies the direct connection between man and his Source—God.

It is easy to make physical contact with another, such as shaking hands. It is somewhat more difficult to experience a meeting of minds. It is rare to experience contact between one soul and another.

When we become deeply aware of the soul of our being and recognize its spiritual dimension, we begin to realize that the body, mind, and soul, acting as a whole, is capable of apprehending the one Source of all.

As our awareness of the Source grows, our spiritual dimension is able to touch the spiritual dimension of others in such a way that we literally are born anew.

III.

Beauty
of
Life

Life, Love,

Living Presence, Movement,

Change, Growth,

Principle of Vibration

Ah, Sweet Mystery of Life!

LIFE IS ANOTHER of those words that we take for granted. If we are asked, "What is life?" we are amused that the question is even necessary. But if we are really pressed to define what we mean by life, we are face to face with a great mystery. No matter how many definitions are put forward or how many attributes of life are discussed, there still remains that mysterious quality of life—that is, life is always more than the sum of its parts.

God is always more than the sum of His parts or manifestations. We can say that about many abstract word symbols such as *balance, beauty, love, infinity, order, harmony,* and so on.

Since all these have a common characteristic, perhaps we could safely say that they are intimately related and in all probability arose out of the same Source. But it is only when we surpass analysis and courageously enter the uncharted areas of metaphysics that we begin to feel or know that mysterious something beyond the observable. *Metaphysical* means "beyond the physical," which can be measured and inquired into; it is the mysterious avenue of the spiritual that defies definition, measurement, description, or captivity.

We are interested in the meaning of life, so let us assume that life always has a spiritual quality that can be experienced but not readily described to another in ordinary language.

We know that life is movement, vibration, growth, change, assimilation, interchange. The life of any living thing in the universe first manifests, then grows to maturity, and slowly recedes to another plane called death. But through all these ceaseless changes there is constancy. Constancy through change is a relatively unknown characteristic of life. In spite of constant changes, something within the living entity never changes. What is it?

We have no terms for it that would be acceptable to all of us. But it has been referred to as God, Source, Christ, Living Presence, Essence. Any term will do as long as we realize that each of us has buried within us something that will never, never change—something that we can seek and find even though it will be difficult to talk about.

We could just as easily call this our soul quality, which has long been associated with the spiritual dimension. When the soul of me recognizes the soul of you, we experience ineffability. We are in the realm of nonmeasurement, but we do not argue about its existence because we go beyond faith or belief into the more certain area of knowing. This is a knowing that needs no proof.

The realization of God-essence within ourself is a discovery of major import. But the realization that the same God-essence exists in every living thing in the universe is a mating that produces cosmic fireworks.

Life is. Life pulsates. Life penetrates. Life is to love. Ah, that is the secret! The beloved does not have to be totally understood, but must be completely accepted. When life and love interact, even the cosmos stands in awe.

Watch Your Step

IT APPEARS EACH of us is eternally on our own staircase. Every action—whether it is directed toward ourself or to the objective world—is a step-by-step movement. It matters not what we call the step—a phase, stage, hour, plateau, crest, trough, valley, peak, child, adult, birth, death.

When we observe any "thing," we are seeing it at some stage of its development. We only snap a picture that freezes the action or change at a particular moment of time. The object pictured, however, does not stop its progression.

Life as we know it spontaneously emerges from a state of being that we call by many names—God, Void, the All, Cosmos, zero, stillness. Out of the state of being arises a state of becoming. This state we call life. Each particle of the cosmos, whether it be an atom or a person, is subject to universal laws that govern its type, quality, and span of life.

Everything is born, matures, dies.

Everything appears from the invisible, reaches

its zenith of visibility, and returns to the invisible.

Everything has wave action.

Everything is cyclic.

Cyclic—this means that an atom or a person appears, disappears, reappears!

It is an eternal ongoing—an upward, step-by-step spiral motion. Whether we like it or not, we are individually at some step on our staircase. When we are conscious of our state of constant change, we can choose to cooperate with the rhythm of life—or not.

Let us consider each step of our staircase as a step to awareness—awareness of life, awareness of our development, awareness of the possibility of fulfillment. We have the fantastic ability to choose to a large extent the rate and nature of our development. We can stand still and be satisfied with our present height. We can go down—or we can go up.

"In my Father's house are many mansions." If you visualize the stairway in a tall building, you will realize that it is essentially spiral, with a large step or platform at every floor. As you begin at the bottom it is rather easy going, but you soon begin to tire from the exertion of climbing. You can rest at any point and begin to climb again, or you can enter a floor and comfortably stay there and not make the effort to climb higher. As you climb you can look back down the stairwell and get dizzy from the height. Or you can look upward and feel the excitement of challenging one mystery after another!

The point is, we need to know that our life resembles a spiral staircase and that we can choose to make the effort to climb higher and higher on the scale of awareness. Each step higher marks a degree of achievement; but, more important, it marks a step closer to full awareness of who and what we are.

Never should we allow a day to go by when we do not "Lift our eyes to the fields, for they are ready to harvest."

The answer to this great mystery of God lies within our grasp, if we choose to cooperate with the flow of life and allow ourself to continue our journey to the stars.

Spring of Life

AS I SIT in my study writing, it is a blustery March day with intermittent snow, ice, rain, and dark clouds. Winter is in full swing—life seems hidden from view. The blackish silhouettes of trees against the gray sky demand that one see the basic form of the tree. The structure stands naked yet sturdy against the power of the winter blast.

If one looks closely, though, he sees the buds are already set upon the branches for the oncoming spring of life.

Life—that mysterious wonder of God that at this point in time has retreated but left its calling card of renewal in the newly set buds. The rhythm of life is somehow forced upon us, if we but allow ourself the luxury of a few moments of quiet observation. Incipient life is everywhere, for those with eyes that see and ears that hear.

The pulse-beats of our own heart prove the presence of life within us, but we have to look more closely for its presence outside our window in midwinter. Our silent observation reveals life is present but mysteriously inactive. Yet deep within our being we sense the preparations for the explosion of the spring of life.

Why, we ask ourself, does life assume the rhythm of on and off? The answer to this question lies buried within. Life is. Life pulsates. Life penetrates. Life is to be loved. Ah! that is the secret! When life and love interact, even the cosmos stands in awe.

The spring of life begins in March and with it our love of life renews itself. It is easy to fall in love with life when we see the first crocus stand erect and shout that a new surge of life is here.

At this time of year I can put a seed in my garden and in a few days it will burst forth with exuberance to live and grow and be admired by those who have discovered love in the spring of life.

What a wonder it is to be alive, to be aware, to be a part of this spring, to realize that love is the catalyst for life and the essence of God is everywhere awaiting our discovery.

The spring of life encourages us to recognize the infinite combinations possible when we mix life and love in God's crucible. When we finally realize that each entity so produced reaches for individuality and thus cries for attention, we can only shed tears of joy that we are so wondrously made.

The Crowning Achievement

YESTERDAY I WENT hiking on the Appalachian Trail in western North Carolina. Today I am still in awe of the experience. In the quiet splendor of the woods, far away from the noise of the cities, I found again (as I always do) a resonance with the composite vibration of the natural life around me. Once again I was in the cathedral of the woods.

Here the choir is enchanting. Its choristers are plants, insects, birds, and animals, and their music is composed by nature. A symphony of light, sound, touch, and fragrance surrounds and is sensed by anyone who desires to experience it.

A thought that persisted throughout the hike: Every form of nature is unique! Not a leaf, not a flower, not a centipede is exactly like its counterpart.

Imagine a billion unique forms vibrating their life forces—inspiring, expiring, growing, radiating—each individual form crying out for its own uniqueness and yet singing or playing in a larger symphony of organization far beyond its range of consciousness. Each plays its own note on its own instrument, perhaps unaware of its importance in the total score of the music.

Each note is necessary somehow to the whole and would be missed were it not sounded. When one realizes that he is only one note in a trillion notes, he is humbled by the complexity, the size, the wonder of it all. And yet when one realizes that his note is essential to the whole, he becomes ecstatic and sings the "hallelujah chorus" with a joy beyond understanding.

We are able at times such as these to encompass an entire swing from the microcosm to the macrocosm and consciously be aware of the awesome beauty of all.

Even though we are not the whole, we somehow know that the whole would not *be* without us! We recognize the beauty of our individuality and intuitively know that the whole is always greater than the sum of its parts. This is the supreme mystery of the universe.

We are part of a larger organization that extends to infinity, and yet we can be consciously aware that each part is needed and is gently connected to every other part.

To be consciously aware that this is so is the crowning achievement of being alive.

Life Is Music

THE CHANGE OF seasons has always been a welcome experience. We are, whether we realize it or not, highly cyclical individuals, and something deep within us responds to each minute change of the length of the day.

Rhythmic cycles are so much a part of us that we literally take them for granted; but when the rhythm is upset we can clearly detect it.

Daily, out of the darkness of night, the light of morning appears, reaching its zenith at noon, diminishing in the afternoon; then darkness returns.

Annually it is winter, spring, summer, fall, and back to winter.

In a lifetime it is birth, growth, maturity, death.

One phase of the cycle imperceptibly becomes another phase, and we recognize their separation only because we have learned to name several different segments of the entire cycle. In reality it is a continuous change from moment to moment, forever repeating itself in millions upon millions of different cycles within cycles. The closest word-concept we have for this eternal activity is *music*.

Reality is movement expressing itself in waves superimposed upon waves. It is the music of the spheres. Wave motion is primary to existence.

Music is the sound of wave motion. Within the realm of that which we call music are the qualities of rhythm, harmony, key, pitch, tone, timbre, timing, and many, many others. But one thing we should observe about music and its source, wave motion, is that time is inexorably a part of the wave cycle. The "no time" condition exists only in the interstices between waves, and the crest and trough of the wave. Sound is born out of silence. Silence is the womb of sound. Silence balances the activity that arises out of it.

The significance of all this is that we have great power to alter the condition of the music being played within us and around us.

In reality, we choose the characteristics of the music being created within the instrument of our body and mind. We can choose to create musical waves that will harmonize, neutralize, or destroy other music in our immediate environment.

If our power is not strong enough to change the condition of the environment, we still have the choice of moving to another location that is in harmony with us.

We are the composer, the director, and the orchestra of our own symphony. We have the choice of what we wish to create, how it is to be played, and with what instrumentation.

Obviously, since each of us is a living symphony of musical wave motion, we affect the atmosphere of each other when we come within each other's range of reception. Also, *everything* within our range of perception is sending out its own musical vibrations, so when we listen for people-music, animal-music, plant-music, inorganic-music, we may experience cacophony, dissonance (noise), tolerable but not inspiring sound, harmony, and (on rare occasions) ecstasy.

If we realize that we can create on our own the type of music that thrills us and actively choose the sounds we will accept from the outside environment, we can readily see the immense power we have to create our soul's desire for beauty, harmony, ecstasy . . . music captured for an instant.

IV.

Beauty
of
Action

Polarity, Choice,

Center of Balance,

Doing, Changing, Direction.

At the End of the Rainbow

HOW DOES ONE find his way through the maze of the present-day world? When we look at the self-help books, we may get the feeling that we are inadequate in just about everything—how to get rich . . . how to be a success . . . how to be a good wife . . . how to be more masculine . . . and so on. But it seldom occurs to us to question whether or not, when we achieve these things, we will be content, feel secure, be at peace.

I have observed many people who have what appears to be the greatest quality for achievement: a single consuming purpose, ideal, or goal. Yet often when these people reach the top, they find themselves still empty, confused, unfulfilled.

On the other hand, I have seen a person who is often considered an "underachiever" but who is balanced, content, at peace with himself and others, and who genuinely radiates a love and a zest for living. Usually you will discover that such a person has been able to balance his desires and so has retreated from extremes of any kind.

Often we are led to believe that, unless we have extreme ambitions to achieve, we are losers. It seems to me that the evidence is to the contrary. Those who choose to be extremists also choose a very narrow, treacherous path. A few of them may realize their dreams, only to find that they have achieved their goals at the loss of almost everything else they treasure.

Whenever you find a person who *must* "get to the top" at any cost, you usually find beneath the surface a troubled person.

As in everything that man can describe, there are exceptions. Occasionally, out of the millions born on this planet, we find one who is born with exceptional resources for living and thinking, one who can do many things well and shift easily from one activity to another. He is fantastically adaptable to life; he is not narrow or pathologically ambitious. Unfortunately, such a person is rare.

Most of us have the potential to be well-developed, intelligent men and women, living a balanced life to the fullest without "cracking up" in the process.

The highly competitive person who has to be the best, get there first, run all the time, be loved by everybody, get rich in money only, has a difficult time finding balance in life.

It seems wiser for us to seek to find a way through life that offers joy, intimacy, satisfaction, and a real understanding of what it means to enjoy life. Let's live now—today—in such a way that death will seem just another milestone along the way and not an unwelcome interruption of our "foot race" with life.

The Way We All Must Go

WE HAVE OFTEN heard the wise course of action suggested by Shakespeare:

This above all: to thine own self be true. And it must follow, as the night the day, thou canst not then be false to any man.

Being true to oneself is apparently one of the most difficult things to do—so few people are able to achieve it!

Few people understand the meaning of the statement. The development of maturity required to appreciate the freedom to be oneself is so very rare. Free souls with the independence necessary to follow their own narrow path of spiritual enlightenment are both a curse and a blessing to mankind.

Those who are being true are often a threat to mediocre persons. Intuitively, every person secretly desires freedom and fulfillment, but most people lack the commitment, conviction, or courage to achieve these. When we find a person who is being true to himself, we often feel a deep sense of guilt for not doing it ourself. Those who persist in going their own way in spite of dire warnings from their fellows are sometimes crucified for their audacity.

Without these creative Truth seekers, mankind would still be in the primeval darkness. A free soul who knows God within, listens for His message, and acts upon His guidance constantly creates new dimensions of life in the universe.

Each of us has the opportunity to discover his real Self, and then to be true to that discovery. The quality of all our expression is in direct proportion to the degree of awareness of Self, but this awareness must be put into action. Dreaming can be most pleasurable, but only when the dream manifests on earth can it be shared by others, who can then be lifted to the same plane of spiritual communion as its creator.

Daydreaming about being a free and independent spirit is evanescent. We are required to struggle against conformity, security, and apathy if we are to rise to our potential greatness of individuality. We are one with the Source of all—we partake of its power, beauty, and love only if we choose to partake!

Why are we so afraid to be what we intuitively know we can be? What is it that keeps us from becoming what we know we could be?

Each of us must answer these questions for

himself. We must diligently search the depths of our being and discover our abilities, which are dormant only because we are fearful of the unknown. *We can.* We must, if we are to be true to ourself, which is ultimately the way we all must be.

When we insist upon our divine right to be ourself we become a blessing to others. Only in this way do we *not* beg, borrow, or steal what is not rightfully ours. When we claim our divine inheritance, we also simultaneously receive the means through which it can manifest into the light of earthly reality.

We become a blessing to the world in the measure of our physical, mental, and spiritual maturity. When we knowingly become co-creators with God, our creations are eternally satisfying to all people everywhere.

The highest achievement is spiritual fulfillment. Only when we are being true to the highest within us are we capable of understanding the import of our actions!

Why Is It Difficult to Choose?

ONE OF THE difficult problems we face when we try to make a case for creative choices is the fact that most people believe they are already making too many choices. However, if we look closely at the choices being made daily by almost everyone in our culture, we find that they are mostly *unconscious* and preconditioned. Moreover, they are mostly defensive or protective in nature because of the tremendous amount of stimuli reaching each person. The response to this stimuli is almost wholly automatic and not of our conscious choice.

Obviously we do not wish to make every choice come under our conscious control, because there are many processes that are beautifully handled by the automatic mechanisms of our body. On the other hand, we do not want the whole of us to become automatic. We must guard certain areas of choice from becoming automatic, to insure our freedom as an individual. Those minor processes which are usually automated, we gladly allow, but those processes which direct our total organism toward purpose, meaning, love, and achievement, we certainly wish to maintain control over.

Most people are asleep; not in a literal sense, but in the sense that they are not aware of their innate ability to choose and so design their own life style. A high proportion of people walk around in a trancelike state—acting, reacting, without any real control of their affairs.

What produces this condition? When a hypnotist wishes to put a person in a trance, he uses the method of focusing the subject's attention on a repetitive action, such as a swinging object. He says, "Watch the watch," or he keeps repeating over and over and over, "You are getting sleepy." This constant repetition and focused attention produces the trance. We experience thousands of similar repetitive stimuli each day of our life. Here again, in order to live, we must receive a certain number of messages from the outside to keep us informed of possible danger or of constructive activities. But when outside penetration reaches the level often found in today's world, it becomes pathological; it is disease-producing.

One of the greatest health-destroying forces extant today is *overstimulation*.

If you can imagine yourself as a giant pincushion, with a thousand people sticking pins into your skin, you will have some conception of the tremendous problem of overstimulation of our nervous system today. It is a well-known physiological and psychological principle that if we are subjected to the same stimuli often and long enough, we build up a tolerance to the stimuli, and we become unaware that the stimuli are still penetrating our defenses. What is frequently overlooked is the fact that the nervous system does have physical limitations. Also the constant repeating of the stimuli is hypnotic, and as a result this trancelike state produces automatic responses until the person finally loses his ability to control such responses.

It is becoming increasingly difficult for us to make conscious choices, because we are being hypnotized daily and kept in an automatic condition that is below the level of awareness and prevents creative choice.

It is an agonizing thought that out of the billions of people on this planet Earth, only a very small percentage can still choose creatively, consciously, and freely.

However, it *is* possible to reassume control of our ability to choose, and live gloriously on our own terms. Wake up and live!

To Church or Not to Church

SOME OF THE most spiritually advanced people I know rarely go to church. On the other hand, many in the same category do go to church regularly. (Notice that I said "spiritually advanced," not "religious.")

At some point in our life, we should ask ourself, "What should I expect from a church?" We should also examine our motives if we do or do not go to church. Simply stated, we could ask: "Why do I need to go to church?"

The church was made for man, not man for the church. Throughout the ages churches have been built and maintained to fill spiritual needs. Some churches today adequately fulfill those needs for many, many people; others do not.

Let's look at some of the spiritual needs a church can provide.

It can provide sanctuary—a consecrated place of refuge from the strife of the everyday world. Everyone needs sanctuary whether he finds it in a forest or in a beautiful chapel.

The church provides ready-made methods of worship, prayer, and discipline. Each of us needs discipline in living.

The church administers rituals. The need of some ritual in our life is still deeply embedded within us whether we recognize it or not—rituals such as baptism, communion, and marriage. In modern times ritual has been looked upon by many as being primitive and therefore un-sophisticated. It *is* primitive, but if you think you can live without ritual, examine your feelings the next time you light a candle for a romantic dinner for two, or even when you enjoy your newest flower arrangement.

The church provides spiritual education for us and our children. Most of us desire to awaken in our children the awareness of spiritual nature. This is intuitive in us, or perhaps we could say in-stinctive. We sometimes exaggerate this need for our children when we feel guilty about not having developed our own individual spiritual dimen-sions; however, many sensitive children have been severely damaged by mediocre Sunday schools where an attempt was made to "put the fear of God in them" and fill their minds with illogical, unproven, so-called fundamentals.

We are born with a spiritual sensitivity. The degree or amount of this sensitivity varies throughout a wide range. The more spiritually sensitive we are, the more danger there is in forced feeding of religious concepts.

The real purpose of the church and its ministers is to awaken, nurture, develop, and finally release the spiritual dimension of men and women. Unless each worshiper develops to spiritual maturity, the church has failed to fulfill its function. The most important part of this process of spiritual illumination is release. Every animal in the world releases its young when they are mature enough to survive alone.

The greatest error that church organizations have made is to unnaturally bind their followers to them by any means necessary (and the "means" at times have reached terrible extremes).

Each individual has the right to experience his own spiritual dimension fully, without outside control of any kind. The church merely sets the stage on which the play of spirituality can take place. When the church attempts to become the playwright, the play, and the audience, it has forfeited its right to exist.

The mystic quality we are born with is our most precious possession. As we become aware of it, everything in the world is beautified by it. It matters not whether we are an elder in the church or one of its ministers; if we have not the gift of spiritual awareness, we have nothing of importance.

When we have developed spiritually, then we

can truly choose "to church or not to church"!
Either way, we will make our own important contribution to humanity because spiritual illumination radiates.

Each of us has the capacity to be a holy person.

V.

Beauty
of
Nuance

Discrimination,

Sophisticated Choice,

Principle of Rhythm,

Flowing, Sensing,

Feeling, Cycles

Look at Me!

IT HAS OFTEN occurred to me that everything in the universe is crying out to be recognized! Apparently each object has its own identity and wants to express it.

Perhaps we could argue about whether this is true of inorganic matter, but it seems to me that the evidence is indisputable when we observe organic or living entities. Why else would plants respond to green-thumb people—those who seem to be able to grow anything? The love of the gardener is somehow transmitted to the plant, which receives it and responds in every way it can.

We all have observed domestic animals responding more to one person than to another. My theory is that animals know those of us who care enough to give attention to them as individuals. When we consider an animal as a class—*i.e.,* dogs in general—the response is minimal. But when we single out a dog and name her "Lassie," we have recognized an individual dog and she gratefully responds with love and affection.

On the human level we sometimes see terribly wounded people who for some reason have not been given attention or love when they needed it, have not been recognized or revered, have not been able to express themselves. A person's response to such starvation can be violent behavior, which is one way of attracting attention; or a retreat from life, causing the person to shrivel up like a prune.

If you accept my theory that each of us is crying out for love and attention, and that the way we get attention is by expressing ourself, it follows that we must concern ourself with the nature of the expression.

If we want to express ourself and be loved by others, we must first allow others the same privilege. We must focus our attention on specific people, at least long enough for them to know we care. Our message of love is received and then transmuted to love energy, which can be directed to any object in the universe. As each object receives love, it in turn potentiates love and retransmits it.

Love begets love. As we express the fullness of our heart we simultaneously open ourself to receive from other sources. Without this constant interchange of love energy, the heart deteriorates.

At last we begin to see that what the prophets said is literally true: Every particle in the universe is indissolubly linked to every other particle in the universe. There is a unity or oneness. If we interfere with the communication between the particles, we temporarily cut ourself off from the very source of our existence.

No one can order us to love . . . but without love, we cannot long survive.

The Art of Living

MOST OF US have had peak experiences that could be described as partial spiritual illumination. For example, haven't you felt something beyond yourself, yet at the same time something special within yourself, when you were viewing a beautiful scene such as a sunset? Haven't you felt "goose flesh" break out spontaneously when beauty pervaded your being for a brief moment in time? Haven't you felt inadequate to describe some special moment in your life with another person? Haven't you felt a wave of vibration throughout your body at a certain trill of music? Can you remember what a miracle you experienced when you touched the skin of a newborn baby?

Whether you realize it or not, all such moments when you transcend your ordinary self for a brief span of time are spiritual experiences. Admittedly they have physical and mental aspects, but since we are not disembodied spirits our experiences always will be physical and mental! This is the area where a spiritual extremist may feel guilty about his body and mind. The senses of the body and the thoughts of the mind are the keys to the kingdom of the Spirit. Don't throw them away! Learn to use everything you have to fulfill your destiny.

The art of living consists of knowing what to keep and what to throw away as excess baggage. Living the beautiful way of life calls for a discriminating choice of the wonders at your beck and call. You choose those wonders that build you up, not those that tear you down. You choose only those things that fulfill your own very special needs. You have become a master in the art of being and building yourself. You always maintain a firm hold on the rudder of your life ship. But you must steer a course toward the goal of your choosing. You recognize the essence within you and selectively seek its reunion in the world about you.

You become an eternal optimist. You recognize the difficulties of the journey, and you increasingly envision the beauty of the destination. The more your awareness of the infinite beauty increases, the less the rigors of the journey concern you. You accept the hardships, but you are so filled with awe at the beauty that they appear to be of slight importance.

So, as Browning said, we release "the hidden

splendor" and claim our right to it.

Most of the time we are so involved with the "important issues" of life that we miss the wonders of the simple and obvious directly in front of us. Even though you must keep your eye on your own star, you must balance yourself by watching your earthly footsteps, lest you miss the opportunity to discover the hidden splendors of the morning glory at your feet.

There is more beauty, more pure joy within the reach of your hands than you could have dreamed possible. Somehow we have been led astray from what is right before us. You can find serenity plus beauty in a single leaf of a tree, in lichen on the side of a rock, in the perfume of a single flower, in the sound of a whippoorwill, in the closeness of the woods, the openness of the meadow, the vastness of the sky over the counterpoint of its clouds, in the sounds of the city, the purr of a cat, in the intimacy of a loved one. All this, and more, is made for you! Can you truly be too busy, too acquisitive to take to yourself that which will always go with you, in whatever life becomes?

We are rich beyond our imagination. There is too much! We can't contain it all. Observe with discrimination that which fulfills your purpose for being. You have a purpose.

We need to develop a condition of dynamic balance wherein we can take positive control of our life, achieve a new image of ourself, and finally so fill ourself with the beauty of love that we can freely and truly begin to give ourself away. Unless we learn ultimately to share our awareness of what is, we will explode into our own emptiness.

Walk, Don't Run

GREAT TRUTHS COME to us at times from the most unexpected places. It seems that the only requirement for the reception of a new insight is an open mind. In our daily activities it is quite difficult to be receptive as we noisily and fretfully engage in our tasks at hand. Most of us are subjected to haste, tension, and confusion.

Some years ago I discovered that what I wanted most in life was a greater spiritual understanding. I read mountains of books, and after sifting through most of the concepts, I realized that most of those who really had firsthand spiritual experiences were saying, "Explore yourself, control yourself, give yourself."

I kept asking myself, "How can I explore myself in such a chaotic society as we have today?" I found most churches lacking the answers I was seeking. Slowly, with further sorting of ideas, I discovered that most of the spiritual giants of the past had had the same difficulty and found it necessary to go "apart awhile" to find solace and to rediscover themselves. Most of the mystics had gone to the most likely place of peace—the woods or the country areas.

I began walking alone in the woods as often as I could. At first I had great difficulty controlling my thoughts—I just rehashed the day; and as I walked, I discovered that I had absolutely no control over this ceaseless flow of thought. I soon realized that control was essential. I made a pact with myself—at the beginning of my walk. I would under no condition bring my daily tribulations to this period of walking and meditating. I wanted just to be—to be open. I wanted to quiet my thinking during these walks and to be aware of the universe around me.

As time went on, these walks began to awaken within me powers of perception that I had never before known. I began to see, hear, smell, feel as never before. I was able to feel increasingly a peace, a warmth, yes, even a love that I had been missing because of all my haste to "take thought."

Soon I became aware of a transcendent state of being that literally permeated the natural world. As I more and more persisted in these walks, I felt that I had discovered something of ineffable importance. Thoughts and solutions that had eluded me in my daily work flowed into my mind so easily and effortlessly that I understood the way to real knowledge was first to seek the peace of my inner self and then to open myself to the all-pervading life stream that flows uninterrupted in everyone. I saw that as we wind ourself up so tight with concentrative forces, we actually prevent the return flow of energy from the timeless source within us.

What a discovery this was! I need only walk in the woods to find myself! I could exercise my body, relax my mind, and recognize the Source of my being all at the same time. In a sense, this entire activity was a new way of prayer for me. The walk itself became "praying without ceasing." I felt at-one-ment with my Creator. I felt as though I were His co-creator as new insights appeared from this inner Source.

The realization slowly dawned upon me that the real secret of fulfillment is in the balancing of that which we receive from our Source with the equal force of giving ourself wholly back to the Source of all. The soul is nurtured by the dynamic interchange. It is the breath of life. What message do you get, my friend, when you take a solitary walk in the woods?

One Step Beyond

THERE IS A fine line between grossness and beauty. The apprehension of beauty requires development in the observer. As one develops from infancy, there is a process of refinement, of discrimination, which is natural unless it is obliterated by other forces.

Fortunate is the child who has one or more persons close to him who are highly developed spiritually. Just the nearness of such a person affects the sensitivity of the growing child. A spiritually-developed person constantly challenges those near him, silently or verbally, to see, hear, and feel more.

Once this latent ability is sparked into life, it continues to grow and manifest itself in a myriad of experiences. Life becomes a continuous process of unfoldment of untold beauty and harmony.

Unfortunate is the one who must find and develop this latent ability without outside help. It is possible, but much more difficult.

If you study your friends, you will recognize those who seem to seek out and appreciate the beautiful, and also those who seem to be moved only by grossness. The latter seem to understand only high intensity, largeness, heaviness, loudness, and so forth—always the extremes. They apparently are unaware of delicacy, gentleness, fineness, microsize.

If after close scrutiny of yourself you find that your process of refinement has been arrested, every effort must be made to regain and revitalize this innate quality. You can discriminate consciously between grossness and refinement if you choose to. You may need to change friends, or seek out those who can help you experience on a higher plain.

The differences of interest between two persons can be striking. During World War II, I was stationed on the windward side of the island of Oahu, at Kaneohe Bay. A friend and I were given liberty to go to Honolulu for a weekend. Honolulu is on the leeward side of the island, but one must go through the Nuanhu Pali (a mountain pass) to reach it. We took a bus that wound around the precipitous mountain roads at a hairraising speed. It was the custom for the bus to stop at the top of the Pali for about fifteen minutes so everyone could enjoy the beauty. As we got out of the bus and walked to the edge of the road, the view toward Kaneohe Bay was the most breathtaking that I had ever experienced. The winds swirled through the pass, and we had to struggle to keep a sound footing, but the struggle was worth the reward of seeing the lush countryside reach down to the deep blue sea. I felt almost heavenly. How could something be so beautiful? I was transfixed by the beauty and unaware of anything but the scene spread out before me.

Suddenly I was awakened by my friend's loud insistence that we must return to the bus posthaste or we would miss the delights of the bars of Honolulu. I turned toward him with surprise beyond words. He hadn't been affected by the Pali! He thought only of his first drink in Honolulu. How different we can be from one another! On the surface we were quite similar, but obviously we had different inner development. The line of demarcation can be fine, but it does make all the difference.

In Kyoto, Japan, there is a famous Zen monastery with a sand-and-rock garden of exquisite symmetry, harmony, and beauty. It was composed as a solid symphony. Each rock is so placed as to complete the composition. If only one rock were moved a few feet, the entire harmony would be destroyed. The placement is mysteriously correct, and only those who see know the difference. One misplaced note in a symphony creates noise instead of beautiful music.

You can, if you will, take one step beyond!

In or Out?

WHENEVER I HAVE need of regeneration of
body or mind I go either to my friends, the trees in
the woods, or to the seashore. In both instances I
avoid as many people as possible—not because I
dislike them, but because they are so much with
me in my daily life that the balance of solitude is
needed during these rest periods.

The vibrations that I receive when I open myself
to the sea seem more universal, less personal, than
those I receive from the woods.

The woods give to me their intimate feeling of
individuals—a tree, a lichen, a mushroom—each
with a different frequency of vibration. But each
is an entity like me with structure, movement,
growth, decay. Each entity appears to be a musical
note in the symphony of the woods, harmonizing
to produce a composite wave of vibrations that
soothes, yet entices my soul to seek its spiritual
mystery.

The woods give to me (and I receive) their

message in the measure of my receptivity to or awareness of their treasures. They heal my wounds from the outside in.

The sea is different! It is open, vast—impersonal. As I sit quietly by the shore I feel myself letting go—giving out—vaporizing like water—forgetting my body, losing my thoughts—expanding, expanding—losing personality. I give myself freely without fear of loss.

Concentration is impossible. Meditation is not needed. Contemplation fades into nothingness. The sea is reclaiming its own and I do not resist its drawing power.

As I lose consciousness of myself to the sea, my body normalizes its rhythm, since expanded thoughts are no longer upsetting its natural harmony. My intellect with its insatiable curiosity is stilled, allowing the all-pervasiveness of Spirit to spread gently throughout my being. Nature is automatic when the mind is at rest. Body and mind heal themselves when left alone. The spirit of the sea permeates. It spreads over one's being as the surf rolls over beach sand.

I remain lost to ecstasy for an indeterminate time. Sometimes a loud noise brings me back to my body-and-mind consciousness. Sometimes I awake as from a natural sleep. But either way the feeling of deep comfort and peace lingers, sometimes for days. Such a spiritual experience is of the greatest significance.

In the woods one can transcend oneself by receiving the message of other entities and so join the song of the soul of nature—or Spirit. It is taking in to the point of overflowing.

At the seashore one gives oneself up to wholeness—allness—oneness—loses his body-and-mind awareness, only to gain ecstasy, if only for a moment.

You can find your Source of being by taking in—receiving—until the zenith is reached and you go over the top.

You can find your Source of being by giving yourself away until all is given and you pass into the ecstasy of Spirit.

The dual poles—in and out—merge into one. You are home!

Fear of Silence

A FEW YEARS ago I regularly conducted *silent* walks through the woods at Unity Village, for groups of retreatants from all over the United States. Before attempting such an audacious task as asking retreatants to be absolutely still for an hour or more, I found it necessary to lecture for an hour *before* the walk in an attempt to demonstrate to them the value of silence.

I had discovered that even though a person might say he was accustomed to "entering into the silence," very few individuals really knew or understood the concept of silence. I found that silence to most people meant a form of prayer wherein one would repeat denials or affirmations to himself, or would listen to another person doing the same. Rarely did they experience stillness of thoughts or of words.

Most people really have a fear of silence. Noise is so much a part of our modern culture that in those rare moments of true silence, we experience a feeling of anxiety because it is so strange.

During a recent period, my wife and I lived in a house on a busy highway. It was extremely noisy, and living there was a most difficult challenge to meet. At that time we were given a golden retriever puppy; during her first few months of life she was exposed to an almost constant din. One evening when we were in the living room, everything suddenly became absolutely still—no cars, no trucks, no airplanes. It was as if suddenly the world had stopped buzzing. Each of us immediately awoke from the noise to a feeling of sudden anxiety. What had happened? The dog, who was sleeping on the floor, awoke as if an intruder were coming; she went to the window, obviously puzzled. What was this new experience—a silent world?

In a few moments the noise returned with full fury. What a contrast! What an insight! Most of us have nearly lost our ability to appreciate the quietness, the stillness of our natural world. We have become attuned to background noise as being comforting.

It is obvious that when one is about to lose a capacity or a resource, he must discipline himself in such a manner that he can rekindle the ability to perceive and enjoy it again.

It is difficult for two or more people to walk together through the woods without conversation. It is a capacity almost extinct. We desperately need to listen to the subtle, satisfying vibrations of the woods. The sound of a falling leaf, the wind in the tops of the trees, dew falling to the forest floor—these are unutterable sounds so in contrast to our noisy environment that we apprehend them as terrifyingly silent. But as we retrain ourself to receive these finer vibrations of the silent world, we begin to realize the wonder that surrounds us.

Silence is relative; noise is relative. But the food for our soul is the balancing influence of relative stillness. We all need regular periods of quiet, when the mind is still and the senses are alert to the fine and beautiful silence.

The fear of silence is then replaced by the joy of silence.

We Need an Oasis in Time

IT SEEMS THAT we need an oasis in time. In this busy world of ours seven or eight hours of sleep is not enough to regenerate us fully. Most of us spend sixteen hours a day in stress-producing activity. In our Western civilization we have never learned the gentle art of repose. On the other hand, it appears that the East could learn worldly concern from us. It appears that we are both out of balance.

I would guess that in the United States we have more leisure time than any other people in the world. This means that to provide the survival requisites, we require much less time than any other culture before us. There is a higher percentage of people in our society who can enjoy freedom from a starvation level of existence.

But when we analyze how we use our leisure time, we find that we extend the "wild" activity of our jobs into our free time. One need only look at the large "leisure industry" that has appeared to fill the needs of busy people.

Our so-called carefree homes require an army of appliances to maintain the front that we wish to show the neighbors. We have power mowers, hedge trimmers, electrical tools for every little need. Indeed, the average homeowner has so many so-called freedom-producing aids that he is imprisoned by them. He buys a new gadget to make things easier—he feels an exhilaration the first few times he uses it—then its use becomes routine. But when the gadget fails to work, he becomes terribly distressed. (If you don't believe me—think a moment about your TV.)

Our machines have taken their price—they have removed us from direct contact with the original hand skill (which is always meaningful); they have required much of our time for maintenance and storage and so forth; and when one of them breaks down, it produces a flurry of anxiety. The I-cannot-live-without-it machine has taken its toll. Perhaps we should advertise such as this:

> Buy this machine. It will enslave you
> faster, and you won't have to worry
> about what to do with your free time.

Obviously, I am not against progress in technology as such. It has produced leisure time and removed us from the survival level, but I am trying to make a case for balance and discriminating choice. We mistakenly choose to over-emphasize busyness in all our waking hours, and in our active life have taken no time for serious reflection, which provides the food for our souls.

This was clearly brought out in me not long ago when I took part in a weekend retreat held in a natural setting in Southern California. The leader was Pir Vilayat Khan, a Sufi from India. He not only talked about peace of mind—he genuinely demonstrated it in his person.

The retreat was not one geared to Western style, with minute-to-minute programming, being rushed from one exciting experience to another, and finally collapsing from exhaustion. On the contrary, the retreatants sat informally around the leader, much as we might imagine the disciples sat around Jesus. The leader spoke gently, peacefully, and used words that tranquilized the heart and soul. There were many periods of silent meditation out among the trees. We arose early in the morning to greet the sunrise. The sun became a living source of light and energy to us, for we directed our attention to it and in return we were revitalized.

Somehow the meditation, the quiet talks, and the acceptance of our part in nature washed our souls clean for another unit of time in the world of things. The age-old recommendation, "Come ye . . . apart . . . awhile," became alive with meaning.

Intimacy

IT IS STRANGE that almost everybody is seeking intimacy but only a few of us experience it. Even though it is so universally desired, intimacy is seldom openly discussed or (more important) found.

In other words, we want it but we can't find it. The usual place we seek it or expect to find it is in marriage. But if we really look at the average relationship of marriage, we see that the experience of intimacy is quite rare.

Now you may become disturbed when I say that you desire intimacy but have rarely, if ever, experienced it. You may say, "Oh, I am very close to someone!" But closeness is not intimacy—it is only one aspect of it. What most of us mean by closeness is physical closeness.

You may also say, "I have shared my deepest thoughts and feelings with someone." This is good, but it is still not true intimacy. Besides, after a careful and honest evaluation of your psychological sharing, you will probably find that you presented your best side and left out your most unpleasant aspects. You may have been putting your best foot forward, but somehow intimacy eluded you.

Physical closeness is a common characteristic of intimacy, and so is mental sharing. What then *is* intimacy?

It is a compatible blending by two persons of body, mind, and soul. Blending body and mind is comparatively easy; giving of the soul is quite difficult.

When two souls blend, the physical and mental aspects take on a new dimension. We are no longer self-conscious about our bodies. We are able to reveal our weaknesses as well as our strengths. The physical sense is refined—grossness miraculously disappears. Feelings and thoughts are somehow transmuted to the beautiful, the tender, the gentle. Deep understanding emerges. Each participant becomes much greater than the sum of his parts. He adds a dimension to his being that he could not possibly achieve alone. Perhaps that is why we really desire intimacy: we don't want to be alone. Being half fulfilled is not enough; we desire wholeness, completion, oneness.

I wish I could tell you an easy way to find intimacy, but I can't. All I can say is that I know it exists. It is a reality beyond words of description. It is worth a continuous search. Its discovery is a pearl of great price. It is a communion of souls, second only to union with God. Perhaps if we stop looking so hard for it in the physical and mental realms we will realize that intimacy's hiding place is in the uncharted territory of the soul.

Probably one reason that true intimacy eludes us is that we will not admit to ourself that we really desire it. When we openly admit our desire for intimacy, we allow the law of attraction to begin to work. This takes courage, because of our fear of failure; but then, what *doesn't* require courage in the search for fulfillment?

VI.

Beauty
of
Control

Discipline, Methods,

Techniques, Timing,

Principle of Cause and Effect

Today's High Is Tomorrow's Low

I HAVE BEEN accused of not believing in the oneness of God, because I write so much about the duality of everything that exists.

It is true that my main concern is with reconciling some of the thousands of dualities I find everywhere. It is not true that I am not also concerned with the unity of all things—the oneness, the Source, or whatever you want to call God.

It is my observation, however, that even though we have a name for the Absolute One, we do not or cannot know (except for brief moments of knowing) what the One is. We are not certain that it is either completely with or without motion; some describe this as high vibrations, or fine vibrations. If it were Absolute Silence, that would indicate no motion at all. The only way we are aware of anything, physical or mental, is by sensing motion. Thoughts are things, but things are capsules of motion. Everything is either expanding or contracting. Motion produces sound and light, which in turn is form. It is extremely rare, if it is possible at all, for us to experience formlessness. Perhaps that is why it has always seemed natural for man to see God in his own image (image indicating form).

We are immersed in millions of capsules of motion. Each capsule has a life span, or cycle of existence. Within our own body such capsules are born, grow, and finally recede without our awareness. The obvious example is the blood cells, which are constantly being replaced. Every cell in our body has a life span and is replaced upon death by another. The miracle of miracles is that in spite of this pervasive change, there remains a constancy of form that we call our body.

Even though we seek oneness, we usually experience duality, which is really wave motion. A wave has a base line out of which it emerges (the wave can go above or below this center of motion). From this center it grows to a peak of maximum tension, in sequences of time. It then reverses direction, falls or recedes to the base line, and proceeds until it reaches maximum tension again below center, as we call it—the trough of the wave.

One may ask what has all this to do with our finding God within? Everything! Life consists of reconciling thousands upon thousands of wave actions (reconciling opposites) and exercising as much control as possible over those wave actions.

Today's high is tomorrow's low.

Our job in living is concerned primarily with keeping the action as close to the center as possible. Extreme motion (high peaks and low troughs) may be exciting, but they are also hazardous. Excesses in nature always precede disaster.

Another miracle of nature is that we are able to exercise some control over the many conflicting wave actions in which we are involved. We can control some, but not all. Some cycles are beyond our ability to control (such as the birth, development, and eventual decay of our sun). I have never had much patience with those Truth students who believe that they can change anything that exists merely by taking thought.

Manifest is the word! We are manifested by God action. We develop. We control those actions within our scope or ability. We accept and adjust to those forces beyond us, and experience awe at the entire process.

Connection with the Cosmos

IN THIS AGE of overstimulation, the question arises: How do I know what is true and what is false for me personally? Advice for our every action is abundantly available at every bookstore, newsstand, and library. It is given freely by our friends and associates. It is available for a price from experts of every sort. Just name your problem, and you can find a packaged answer (usually of the textbook variety).

We have been conditioned to depend on others for help and to distrust our own innate ability to intuitively know what is best for us individually. What a pity! How can anyone else completely know our needs and deep desires?

The difference between a genius and an ordinary person is that somehow the genius never stopped listening to his inner voice, and thus escaped the deadly conditioned response of dependency. The genius is inspired and guided by his "genie," which is none other than his own direct connection with the cosmos. All knowledge is available to him who is aware of this power and trusts its capacity to reveal his heart's desire.

When I was a student at a large university, taking an introductory course in psychology, I asked for a discussion of the concept of intuition. I had read the textbook discussion of the general subject of learning, wherein the concept of intuition was dismissed by a single sentence. Yet I deeply felt that the concept of intuition contained many of the secrets of true learning. The teacher was distressed by my interest and summarily rebuked me for bringing it up, since it obviously was not even worthy of discussion.

Intuition is now gingerly discussed in most psychology textbooks, but it is still suspect, primarily because it resists accurate measurement by any known statistical procedure. The pseudoscientist usually shrugs and says, "If you can't measure it, it doesn't exist," or, "If you can't label it, you don't know it!"

The average person today still does not know the difference between intellect and intuition. So-called primitive people were in this respect a lot better off—they knew the difference, and they depended more on intuition than on their memory banks.

Those of us who study what we call Truth at least have been introduced to the concept of intuition. But since we have been conditioned by our educational process, we must vigilantly seek out its true meaning and power for ourself. Usually we listen first to our logical mind (intellect), which is really a great memory bank of stored past experiences, constantly recalled to determine our response to any stimulation, mental or otherwise. How can one be fully alive to the moment if he is imprisoned by the dead past? Spontaneity is of the essence.

It takes "blood, sweat, and tears" to break through the bondage of the intellect and begin to listen quietly to our inner connection with the cosmos—to God. Slowly and sometimes painfully we must differentiate between our predetermined response mechanisms and our intuitive flashes of inspiration. We must constantly ask ourself, "Which is it?" Predictable, at first, we will trust our intellect more; but if we persist we will arrive at the point where we will know the difference. Then we can consciously use our intellect as a tool for implementing the constant flow of fresh new inspirations emerging from the depth of spirit. Eventually we will discover our own connection with the cosmos.

Change without Fear

IT IS A curious thing that most of us resist change with a great deal of effort. Yet when you observe the plant and animal kingdoms, you realize that human beings above all have the greatest capacity for change, adaptation, and continual growth.

It appears that plants and animals are automatically programmed to manifest their characteristics in a very specialized manner. Each species is *prespecialized!* We seem to be free to change ourself, our environment, even our social habits. But we seem to fear change as if it were a sinister thing.

We have the capacity to breathe, but we don't fear it. We can see, but we don't close our eyes in fear.

Perhaps the fear of change is an atavistic condition, since humankind appears to be relatively new on earth. But if we have acquired this unique ability to change, probably at great cost, it would seem that the rewards for this freedom would also be great.

Can it be that we still fear this capacity for change and adaptation because intuitively we know we are still part of nature and yet have the awesome power to change? Do we realize, however dimly, that when we destroy nature's ability to recycle itself, it is as if we were eating our own hand because we are hungry?

It is time that we look squarely at our fear of change, and also at our ability to change and reconcile this conflict. In the world today change is out of control, because we are petrified with fear of the capacity we could use to control it. When we are paralyzed with fear, action ceases and death comes quickly. Only by bold, fully conscious action can we keep our head and our life.

Many of us have submitted to change as a power so overwhelming that we cower as a dog about to be beaten. We know in Truth that mind power can change things. However attractive this possibility may be to us, we seem to forget it completely when we look at the world around us. It is so vast, and we are so small! But if we realize the hermetic axiom—*as above, so below*—we will see that the organization of the individual is exactly the same as that of a galaxy.

To confront change in the world, we must first confront it within ourself—accept it as inevitable, but with awareness of our innate, God-given capacity to control it, organize it, direct it into any channel we wish. If we consciously become aware of our tremendous power to act, fear will vanish. We are most fearful when we are passively awaiting disaster. Only by consciously realizing our abilities and acting them out can we be the masters of our own destiny.

In the microcosm of our own self, we can begin to take control and rise to our full potentiality—to be fully alive on our own terms, to be what we want to be. We can become so engrossed in the activity of fashioning our own life that the fear of change is turned into the power to *be*.

Only by overcoming fear within ourself can we help others, by showing the bright light of wholeness.

Point of No Return

THERE ARE POINTS of time in our life when a sudden irreversible change takes place and we are completely transformed into a new level of experience.

One such point came early in life to each of us. Those who have studied the science of embryology become aware of the great miracles of life. One female cell is irreversibly changed by the acceptance of one male cell, and suddenly both change into one irreversible new entity. This new cell is totally and absolutely different from its previous condition. It has now the capacity to grow into another organism similar to its parents. It has reached a point of no return.

But at this point the embryo's development is limited to proliferating or doubling the number of cells (mathematically, we could say, by exponential growth): one cell becomes two, two become four, four become eight, etc. This rapid growth continues until another miracle occurs, which the embryologists call differentiation. Before this sudden point of cataclysmic change, one small area of this growing ball of cells can be transplanted to any other area and it will accept new cells and grow normally.

But after "differentiation," each area of cells located on this growing ball is now predestined to become a particular type of tissue. In other words, if the cell area is to be a leg, no matter where it is transplanted, it will become a leg. If it is to be an ear, it will become an ear.

These examples of irreversible, cataclysmic change are miracles of life that defy understanding.

If we look at life in general, we find a myriad of such examples in every area—in the development of any wave motion or life cycle that could be one human life span; one sun's life span; or the birth, development, and death of a galaxy.

With each complete cycle, there are many points of sudden, cataclysmic change. With our present measuring devices we frequently overlook these, since a wave motion plotted by the usual two axes on a graph appears to be a smooth, continuous line of development with no apparent changes. (However, life has never been easy to show graphically.)

Here are other examples of these points of change:

1. Crossing a state line, *e.g.,* from Georgia to

Florida.

2. Growth of a city to a point of irreversible change, beyond which point everything suddenly changes into new problems *(e.g.,* New York City).

3. Development of a disease state to the point beyond which the organism cannot regenerate itself.

4. Spiritual illumination of a person—a sudden flash of knowingness that is irreversible and forever changes the individual. He sees where before he saw not. He knows where before he believed he knew.

We could go on and on giving examples from our own life experience, but our object is merely to demonstrate the existence of these sudden changes, and perhaps leave you with a feeling of awe concerning their miraculous power.

Each of us struggles unceasingly, whether conscious of it or not, to understand or to know God. Our preparation time and its nature varies, but inexorably each of us will reach the point of exaltation when we will know and not merely believe. It will be a sudden awakening to a light previously unnoticed. We will then have achieved a level of awareness that will never leave us. This will prepare the way to another level of awareness, which also will come suddenly, by grace, or by . . . what?

Look at It the Way It Is!

FREQUENTLY WE HEAR someone say, "That's not the way it ought to be," or "He should do this or that." In most cases we find that the person who makes such a statement is really imposing his own idealism on some situation. He is disturbed because this life experience is not in accord with his preconditioned concept of the way it should be.

I guess all of us at times fall into this trap of not accepting life as we find it, but rather insisting that life conform to our own incomplete view of it. We are usually so blinded with our concept of purity or perfection that we forget that such conditions do not really exist on our level of observation. Absolute perfection is an illusion; it can only be attributed to our God-essence, not to our manifestation. Who aside from God determines what perfection is?

The attempt to attain perfection is a worthy pursuit for any mature individual—but expecting to find it absolutely could be classed as spiritual pride or false hope.

Another characteristic of extreme idealists is that they frequently talk about how things should be, but rarely act as if they believe it. It appears that the last thing they want to do is observe the existing condition closely. What kind of scientific objectivity would we have if a biologist looked into a microscope and saw a spirochete but loudly exclaimed, "It cannot be there"? The danger is that we can become so obsessed with what *should* be that we can't see what *is*.

There are untold thousands of people who really want to help others but cannot . . . simply because their own vision is so occluded by the mirage of absolute perfection that they lose sight of what the real issue is.

As students of Truth, we set goals toward perfection. One of those goals is attaining maturity. However, we realize sooner or later that a balance is necessary between the ideal and the real. Jesus knew what purity was; but He found little of it in the world, so He set about doing something about it. He healed the bodies and minds of those at hand. He was a doer of the word, and He said, "You will know them by their fruits."

Look at the way it is, and then do something about it!

Can We Accept Our Good?

SO OFTEN WE pray and pray for something to come into our life, and yet when it becomes a reality we cannot fully enjoy it. We have asked that the future become the present without releasing the past, and so residual guilt or a feeling of unworthiness prevents us from accepting our good without reservation. We need to learn to be a gracious receiver as well as a generous giver.

It is a common experience to see a person who apparently gives much of himself but is embarrassed when he is presented with gifts of appreciation. Nature always balances her every action, and if we have freely given, we must clear the way for the return action of our good.

Past experiences should be a stairway to the stars, not a stairway ending in a closet of darkness. Obviously we learn from our errors, and we grow in stature by building upon such experiences and not repeating them. Nature is always nudging us to grow, to mature, and finally to bloom by fulfilling ourself.

Let's think of the common sunflower. It begins as a seed. It is born mysteriously by germination. It struggles to grow. It matures into a full-grown plant, and yet it still has not fulfilled its destiny. It must bloom and when it does, it majestically basks in the sunlight, receiving the warmth, the light, and yes, even the coloration of the sun. It receives the sunlight unabashedly without being bound by the struggle that was required to survive and bloom.

When we struggle to achieve a goal in life; when we are following a deep-felt intuition; when we actualize our most cherished desires—we must not burden ourself with the excess baggage of doubt, duty, guilt. If we are really being true to ourself, we will not be hurting another person. But in the larger sense we give others their opportunity to grow, mature, and bloom. The critical point here is that we must make certain that our goals are pure and that we are not seeking them for simple ego-satisfaction. If we genuinely feel good about what we are doing and then proceed along the road of achievement without compromising our basic integrity, we should not allow ourself to be misdirected by people, places, or things. We should walk steadily toward fulfillment.

If we have opened ourself to guidance from within; if we have been true to our vision; if we have freed ourself from the effect of ego-satisfaction; if we have given freely of ourself—then we should bask in the sunlight and receive our good graciously and thankfully!

We *can* learn to accept our good!

"It Takes a Heap of Livin' "

IT SEEMS THAT just the other day I planted a few seeds of corn in my garden, and now the seeds have turned into plants six feet high. Life abounds in my garden! But I ask myself how high it will continue to grow before it mysteriously stops and begins to decay?

It seems that everything has its limits. What would happen if my corn continued to grow out of control? It appears to be a universal law that everything has a cycle of life and death. Something appears, matures, decays, and finally returns to the Source from which it came. No "thing" is allowed absolute freedom. There are always limits. There are always controls. When an action proceeds faster than is normal for it—its own destruction is also sped up. Each thing has a characteristic rhythm for its growth and decay. When any part of it gets out of control, "like a cancer cell" it begins to speed up the death process.

If we allow ourself the "luxury" of being out of control, we play a deadly game. Children who are not taught how to control or discipline themselves quietly grow into threats to themselves and others. We simply cannot allow ourself the luxury of too much alcohol, tobacco, drugs, anger, hate, interference in the life of others—or even too much air (if we breathe too rapidly we pass out); too much water, and we'll drown; too much concern for self, and we become hypochondriacs; too much concern for others, and we become meddlers.

There is apparently a range of action that is ideal for each person. To live harmoniously, we attempt to adjust our desires to this range. If we break through the physical limits, our body becomes diseased.

Most of us never think about this optimum range wherein we can be balanced yet quite effective human beings. We often harbor the illusion that we are outside the universal law and that we can ignore that law without harm. What a terrible price we pay for our excessive ambition, pride, greed, lust, speed.

All of this also applies to our mental activities as well. Too much thought produces sleepless nights. Many of us are so busy with our intellects that our body and soul begin to decay by default.

I'll say it once again—there is no such condition for a "manifested thing" as absolute freedom! There are limits within which it must move and have its being. A wise person learns what those limits are, accepts them, and joyfully fulfills his purpose for being.

Obviously, there are different limits for each process or idea. We usually overestimate our physical and mental abilities and grossly underestimate our soul qualities.

How does one tell the right action from the wrong action? This takes wisdom, produced by experience. There is no easy answer! As someone said, "It takes a heap of livin' " to know the difference. One method is to choose the actions that are constructive—life-producing—and not the ones that are destructive or death-producing. Most of us know the difference when we are really honest with ourself. So, whether we like it or not, we cannot abandon control of ourself. To live without self-discipline is to become like a racing car at full throttle without a driver.

Timing Is of the Essence

"FOR EVERYTHING THERE is a season and a time for every matter under heaven" (Eccles. 3:1).

Often we become discouraged or even give up entirely after persistent prayer that asks for a specific demonstration. We ask: "Why am I not able to manifest this desire? I have kept my thoughts true to what I want. I have faithfully used the positive approach. I have guarded my attitudes. I have literally done everything I know how to do, and yet I am not able to achieve success."

Upon deep reflection we usually find several reasons why we have not been able to demonstrate in a certain situation, even though we have been productive in other areas. When something we "prayed hard" for is denied us, could it be that the very intensity of prayer has repelled the free flow of the universal power and intelligence? Could it be that unknowingly or perhaps even selfishly we were asking for something that God knows is detrimental to our ultimate good? We think we must have this thing, but infinite Intelligence knows better!

Or could it be that our timing is off? Here is a principle often overlooked in demonstration of Truth. The right idea at the wrong time is usually stillborn. The right idea born at the right time sweeps away all doubt and establishes itself almost effortlessly.

If we are really attuned to our inner guidance and our request is definitely not for self alone, and we *know* it is divinely ordained, then we can relax and let it manifest according to the perfect timing of universal Intelligence. We cannot take the responsibility personally for failure to demonstrate if we have truly been guided in our thinking. The responsibility is God's. We plant the seed, we water it, we nurture it. But we cannot force the growth. We cannot determine its time of germination. We do our part and rest, knowing manifestation is assured at the right time and the right place.

We can learn to attune ourself to the perfect timing of God. Consider an athlete or a musician: timing is of the essence.

Perfect timing is of God. We learn to listen for the delicate message of the right time to do anything. It is a most subtle ability—and those who have discovered even a small understanding of right timing seem to move through life without the ordinary amount of struggle.

Just as you cannot force open the blossom of a rose with your hands, you cannot force manifestation of anything without peril of losing it altogether.

So if you have planted the garden of your desires and have fully done your part, sit back and wait on the Lord God, who alone holds the key to perfect timing.

Forcing is always perilous. Remember that the softness of water can inexorably erode a valley into a deep canyon, perhaps over a million years. But the canyon can also be formed explosively in moments by a giant earthquake. Both produce the same result—only the timing varies. Quick or slow: in the scheme of the universe, does it really make a difference?

When we really understand the relativity of time, we can stop forcing and begin attuning, and truly know that timing is of the essence.

A Time to Sow . . . A Time to Reap

TIMING IS ONE of the important issues of life. It is, however, quite relative. If you are at the right place at the right time, your life will be ecstatic. Conversely, if you are at the wrong place at the wrong time, disaster may occur.

If you swing a tennis racket too soon or too late, the ball goes askew. But if your timing and execution coincide with the position of the ball, your shot hits its mark, and a feeling of exhilaration permeates your being. Perfection in action always produces a feeling of ecstasy.

Obviously we are less than perfect in our worldly expression, but the ideal of perfection draws us onward. Each of us at some time in our life has experienced at least a partial feeling of ecstasy, and once we have experienced it, we want more.

In order to experience true ecstasy all the conditions of life must be in balance. But timing is our main consideration here. Right timing is a quality of balance. It is a dynamic or moving quality and not a static quality. Each moment differs from the previous moment. One way we can tell if our timing is right is by the degree of ecstasy experienced. Ecstasy is the direct reflection of the oneness of God. Therefore, it is the only condition of life that has no opposite. The One becomes two at the beginning of movement or expression.

When the opposite poles of motion are perfectly mated, we have a marriage that results in the ecstasy of the One. The entire play of life is dependent on the movement between the dual poles or opposites. The movement between poles, if plotted on a graph, would show a wave action. Crests and valleys of a wave are usually well defined. Timing consists of harmonizing with this pattern of movement. Every surfer knows that he must mount the wave at exactly the right moment for an exhilarating and effortless ride.

If we wish to make a change in the mode of any action, there is always a time when it is easy and a time when it is almost impossible. The question is: How do we know when the moment is right? By experience, practice, and above all feeling—feeling the ecstasy of the right moment of time! Our entire being must be directed to this moment.

We must become aware that timing is important—that life is fuller and richer when we harmonize with the cyclic forces surrounding us and know when to act and when to be still.

If you have worked long and hard to prepare facts and figures for a presentation by which you hope to get positive actions, and you present it at the wrong time—failure is usually the result. An enormous amount of energy is required to push something through at the wrong time, but at the right time it is seemingly effortless. In the former case you wonder why you had to work so hard.

We have all been at one time or another out of tune—and thus we were bounced around out of control. If only when this happens we can remember the ecstasy of right timing, we will be able to change our life without monumental struggle.

There is a time to sow . . . a time to reap.

You *can* learn to know when that time appears. Right timing is of the essence!

VII.

Beauty
of
Evolving

Fulfillment, Joy, Guidance,

Illumination, New Life,

New Planes of Awareness

Oh, That Spiritual Plateau!

ALONG THE SPIRITUAL path, we often reach a vast plateau that appears endless. After a comparatively rapid climb or period of growth, the sameness of the plateau is in such a contrast to the excitement of the previous movement that we experience extreme frustration, created by doubts that we may never be able to climb further.

It appears that God in His infinite wisdom insists upon frequent rests along the upward journey toward perfect realization.

It is like eating: no matter how appetizing the food, we must stop stuffing it in and allow digestion and then assimilation to take place. We literally cannot, without serious consequences, keep eating continually. However, in contrast to this, when we find ourself on a spiritual plateau, it may seem like eons since our last nourishment. This has been called, in the literature of the mystics, "the dark night of the soul."

During this period, we find that the thoughts

and actions which previously kept our expectations alive seemingly no longer work. Meditation produces little or no insight. Conversation with those we have held in highest spiritual esteem seems insipid. Somehow we feel that God has abandoned us!

When we experience this for the first time, it is extremely painful and apparently hopeless. Each succeeding time it occurs we begin at least to recognize the symptoms and accept it as the natural result of rapid growth—but it is always discomforting.

Yet always, after an indeterminate period of time, and in the midst of our despair, we see a new ray of light that suddenly pours into our soul and immediately lightens the darkness. Despair turns to joy, as we are renewed by this unexpected surge of energy from the Source of our being.

We are (literally) reborn anew.

Not long ago, this happened to me again. After a particularly long, barren plateau wherein it was difficult to feel any spiritual growth occurring within me, a person whom I had not seen for almost four years, and of whose whereabouts I had not the slightest idea, phoned and said she would stop by and say hello.

It was a memorable experience. She is one of those itinerant preachers who scare off most people with their incisiveness and "medicine man" approach. However, on this day, for me, she seemed to have uncanny power in mentioning those painful doubts I had been experiencing, and she repeatedly punched holes without mercy into my carefully constructed "ego suit."

I long ago came to the realization that when on a spiritual plateau, one must be alert for the stimulus that will spark new spiritual insights and abruptly end the plateau experience. It may be a place, a thing, or a person. It has, in my memory, been some of each. You begin to know when God has sent His new messenger to you, and realize the wonder of it.

It is miraculous. Out of this vast universe of time and space, something is sent to you to spark new growth. How personal can God be?

Fortunately, I examined my brief experience with this person carefully, and suddenly realized why I had been unable to escape my present plateau.

The next day, the heavens opened. Everything that I had previously experienced and felt to be dull, boring, and hopeless, reversed its phase and became gloriously alive. The birds sang; every leaf was shimmering with spiritual light; the sky, the deep shadows, became pregnant with new meaning. My timing was flawless. I floated through the ecstatic experience of being reborn again into the awareness of the kingdom of God.

I had reached the end of another period of rest and digestion. The plateau had disappeared.

What Next, Father?

ONE YEAR I had gone to a great deal of work in planting a vegetable garden. It seems that I have always realized many spiritual realities from gardening.

The sweet corn germinated and began rising majestically to the sky—it was well formed and growing vigorously. Then suddenly a violent thunderstorm came up during the night. I arose to see my handiwork lying over on its side—a very distressing sight!

I knew then what a farmer feels when such a disaster takes place. At such a time, one begins to realize how many forces are at work in our life, and how many challenges we have to meet, just as do our plant friends—even when we nurture and love them.

At first I thought the corn would be a total loss, but when I returned from work that day, the corn had already begun to stand up again and by the next day had fully recovered. It never occurred to me when I tried to straighten the stalks by hand and failed that the corn plants could do it by themselves. I should have realized their lust for life and desire to bloom.

So, the plants grew and finally reached over eight feet in height! Then began a prolonged period of drought. Again my fears of failure loomed large, and each day I would tenderly inspect the maturing ears and tassels. The mystery beneath the layer after layer of protective sheaths haunted me. Would the ears fill out, or continue to grow, during such a prolonged drought?

Finally the day arrived when I could wait no longer. I prematurely judged the dryness of the tassel—I had been told that this is how to judge the right time to pick the corn—and unsheathed my first ear of corn. Each kernel was still small and immature but the rows were complete. I picked a few more ears for supper and what a delight it was to taste the fruits of my labor! It was a sweetness that suffused my soul.

My family kidded me about such small kernels on the corn, but I now felt that the plants would fulfill their destiny and that I need not concern myself with further fears of failure. For many weeks we had corn aplenty in the midst of the drought. Apparently the corn had time during its early formation period to put down strong roots, which brought it upright from a strong wind and enabled it to get the necessary supply of water for an extended dry period.

The lesson in this experience seemed clear to me as I enjoyed my achievement. No matter what our goal, we can expect obstacles or resistance. But when we are firmly rooted, we have the strength and the desire to overcome and reap the harvest. The sweetest harvest is that gained when we have given fully of ourself. When we struggle to achieve through our own resources, we quickly feel the danger of failure, but we also deeply experience the ecstasy of achievement. We experience evolution or growth that adds another dimension to our soul.

Perhaps life is not meant to be a continual "bowl of cherries," but rather an opportunity for developing our roots, or our foundation, for higher responsibilities with their concomitant capacity for greater joy.

In spiritual terms, when we root ourself firmly in the Source of our being, God, we are given the opportunities to overcome apparent obstacles; in so doing, we realize more and more the real capacity that we have.

Perhaps this is why so many people get such a "kick" out of making money. It is not so much the money itself, but the ecstasy of achievement. The sad thing is that many of these people are so close to discovering the Source of their being, but have the mistaken thought that money is the source of their joy. They can be so close, yet so far, from the discovery that accumulation of money is only one little harvest in the "farming" of the soul.

So one more lesson has been learned. We can never rest on our past achievements. Rather, we need to ask, "What next, Father?"

The Ultimate Disturber
of Sleep

WHEN WE STUDY the Easter story we can find almost anything we wish. Each event has a rich symbolic meaning for us if we look closely. However, in most of us, the ability to examine anything with close scrutiny seems to be a lost art. We scurry hither and thither, always too busy for inner reflection. We take quick surveys or a panoramic view of life and its events.

As always, nature cries out for balance. If our life is shallow and we are lost in a surface storm, the fault lies in ourself. As Jesus proved, we *can* wrest conscious control of our searching soul and begin to plumb our depths. We can become strong only by exercising our own individual soul resources.

Most of us have been lulled into apathy by the "lullaby of Broadway," whose song promises comfort, security, and pleasure as long as we do not, under any circumstances, seek the Truth within ourself.

The Truth of being is the one thing Jesus knew that set Him free and frightened the daylights out of His contemporaries.

Jesus found the Father of all within Himself and so became aware of the phoniness, the sham, the ignorance of His time. He realized that men and women were unaware of their own ineffable Source of being—that they were still asleep or lulled into that condition by ideologies that imprisoned the mind and so also the body and soul.

Jesus tried to articulate His message of reality to a sleeping audience. He became the ultimate disturber of sleep. He tried to sound the alarm—ring the bell—but the majority of His listeners reacted with resentment. "Why does somebody always have to rock the boat? Put this disturber of sleep to death! His words will destroy everything we hold dear." Oblivion was the order of the day and still is.

As long as the Truth remains hidden, incomplete ideologies can remain matchstick castles, hypnotizing people by their height and glory. And yet we intuitively recognize the danger of one sincere person rapping at the foundations of such fragile erections.

Jesus, along with mystics, saints, and illuminated women and men from all cultures, experienced the fact that the one thing the world of fabrication cannot and will not tolerate is a sincere person who has apprehended the Truth. The

Truth is so simple that its very nature makes an illusion of our so-called everyday world.

We are imprisoned by our own fabrication. We live in a matchstick castle. We have lost the ability to know the Source of our being. But if we take time to reflect on the Easter story and make our own in-depth evaluation, we will discover that out of despair, fear, ignorance, and suffering arose a sincere man who finally triumphed—found the Truth, was crucified for it, and yet rose on Easter morn—as we can, to the pure joy of knowing who we really are and that each of us ultimately will know the Truth that will set us free.

It must be done individually. It cannot be done by outside interpreters who are promising an easy route to the source of Truth.

Awake thou that sleepest—the All in all awaits you!

The Door to Inner Guidance

NEWCOMERS TO THE study of Truth often discover that an inner guidance wells up within them. They seemingly know what to do at each instant. Painfully, though, they soon discover that this supposedly infallible guidance is frequently wrong.

They may be heard to say: "I prayed and prayed for the right outcome—then suddenly I knew what to do, but it couldn't have been more wrong. What happened to me? Don't I know how to pray?"

Several things could be wrong. Enthusiasm over a bright new idea without the experience of its characteristic can produce a false optimism that is more superficial hope than deep inner knowing.

As soon as we grasp the potentiality of Truth, we may jump to the conclusion that we are masters and can go out into the world to save it from its erring ways. We arrogantly assume that a little knowledge (and even less experience) qualifies us to differentiate between the shallowness, the selfishness of our surface mind (which we have been using about 99 percent of the time), and the universal Mind, which uses us.

In the beginning we are unaccustomed to being used. We want to be the flowing water, not the vessel.

As we progress in the quest for Truth, we become less and less pedantic and more and more humble. We begin to realize why the great masters in any field of endeavor develop deep humility and awe for their science. The deeper one goes into anything, the more one realizes its infinite capacity to create wonder.

Those who really know say little or nothing. Those who only think they know shout from the rooftops innumerable half-truths. It is these half-truths borrowed from others that take so much time and energy to sift through.

Real inner knowledge arises from within. Most of our energies, as Truth students, are required in separating the wheat from the chaff. We are constantly wooed by our logical or intellectual mind to accept its subtle conclusions as being guidance from God.

In the early stages of growth, it is easy to mistake selfish desires for deep inner guidance. The question is, "How do I tell the difference between my selfish desires and real inner knowing?" If the answer is given quickly, as if memorized, it is certain to be wrong. The only way anyone eventually knows the difference is by trial and error, and an intense desire to discover the subtleties of one's own mind.

One day you will know that it *is* possible to tell the difference . . . but then you will realize that you are still a neophyte, and have only opened another door to more discoveries. The strange thing about it is that you cannot convey in words precisely how you were able to open the door!

To Know Joy

OFTEN IN THE SEARCH for Truth we find ourself deeply involved in a serious study of intellectual concepts usually called *Truth principles.* We even call ourself a *Truth student,* implying that we will somehow achieve our spiritual goals by academic methods.

Unfortunately, as is so characteristic of our culture, we succumb to the notion that what we are looking for will be found by the arduous method of accumulating and storing for later recall large amounts of data (in this case, information about things "spiritual"). But we are not seeking a Grade-A Information Center! We are seeking wisdom and the joy of *knowing* directly the Source of all intelligence, which we intellectually believe is buried within us.

The gap between faith and belief and the certainty of knowing is enormous. It is sad to see so many serious Truth students going around quoting from this book or that person, and demonstrating to everyone but themselves that they do not *know*—they only have information about!

Perhaps the problem here is in the word *serious*. When we get so seriously involved with Truth principles, we create a tension that prevents Principle from reawakening within us. The forcing of spiritual growth eliminates the spontaneity, the joyousness, and the ecstasy that naturally want to emerge.

If you wish to check up on yourself to see if you are one of these "serious students," ask yourself one simple question: "Is joy flowing forth from me in an unending stream?" If it is, you will not need to justify it by unnecessary study, or by proving you are right, or by entertaining the need for ego satisfactions.

If you are not experiencing this inner joyousness, then this is not the time to become *more* serious in your studies. The answer lies in total acceptance and inner knowing of this one premise: There is only one Power in the universe, one God, one Source—One! Knowing the One is more than simply having faith and believing; it is *pure knowing!*

No one can really tell you how to achieve this pure knowing, but many of us can tell you what not to do. You must know for yourself. It comes imperceptibly as you stop forcing—stop trying to take "heaven by storm." It comes slowly but surely as you begin to give yourself (your little ego self) to humility, to reverence for life, and to the joy of the simple experience of being alive.

Suddenly, one day you will know God in you and simultaneously know God in everything else. Then joy and ecstasy will reign and you will be a radiating blessing instead of an articulating student!

Touch of Eternity

NOT SO LONG ago I was sitting beside a stream watching the water flow rapidly over the rocks. The water appeared to be desperately seeking its source—the sea.

It occurred to me that each of us swims in the fast-flowing stream of life, and that we are drawn inexorably toward our source. If we allow the current to guide us, we seem to be in harmony with the nature of things. Even while going with the stream we have considerable freedom to choose our routes. We can go along side tributaries; we can stay in the main stream; we can choose to stay behind on a sandbar or rock pile.

Sooner or later, though, we will be swept to our destiny by the overpowering current, which at times becomes a torrent and at other times appears not to move at all.

Woe, however, to the one who tries to swim upstream against his destiny—the main current—or to resist every effort of the current to take him "home again." He then has only his own motive power, which he puts against the power Source of the universe. He is unaware of his guiding lifestream and chooses only to resist this mysterious force acting upon him. If he is strong he will make some progress, but the journey gets harder and harder as he goes toward the Source of power.

It appears that each of us has a considerable range in which to choose the manner of travel, the route, the length of time, etc., but we do *not* control the main current (lifestream) of our life's destiny, plan, or orbit.

As I sat there alongside the stream in the woods, a bird suddenly swooped down and snapped up a living bug from the bank. Here was one form of life feeding on another form. Death was all around me and yet life was there, too—the two fit so well together in the woods. And yet out of this seeming violence emanated a vibration that tranquilized my soul. The woods seemed to produce an overtone that soothed me as I sat there and observed the quiet violence of living and dying.

Somehow the details of my everyday life seem to fade into nothingness in the naturalness of the woods. Delicate aromas draw my attention. The sound of the wind gives me a new rhythm. The touch of the brush smothers my worldly ambitions, and I find myself stripped bare of the whirlpools and eddies of my everyday life. A "something"—a composite vibration—calls forth and woos my soul.

Ah! This is living! This is the touch of eternity—life moving in and through me—and I am aware of it! It is neither good nor bad. It is ecstasy! The real me is not on the surface of my planetary travel—it is deep within my core, which responds to my larger orbit and this is beyond my control. I choose to allow my Maker to take me where He will! He chooses the current of the course and He allows me the choice of details. His only requirement is that I never lose sight of Him!

Printed in the United States of America   149-F-4479-15M-12-80